1. Brrr
2. Crystals that make you thirsty
3. Bloodless veins

Answers and Amazing Facts

FOR PAGE 3

1 FROST ON A WINDOW PANE

The lacy, featherlike designs you sometimes see on a window on a cold winter's day are nature's intricate frost patterns. This window frost is created when the water vapor in the outside air freezes as it touches the cold glass. The outside air must be 0°C (32°F) or colder.

2 SALT CRYSTALS

A famous road in history, the Via Salaria, or Salt Road, ran between Rome and the salt mines at Ostia in Italy. The Roman soldiers who guarded this route received part of their pay in salt. It's the name of this ration, the *salarium argentum*, that our modern word "salary" comes from. Today a good employee is still said to be "worth his or her salt".

3 LEAF

Take a quick glance at a leaf. It's easy to think a leaf is a simple part of a plant, but all leaves perform an important function. The leaf uses the energy of sunlight to make food for the plant in a process called photosynthesis. The veins you see in the picture transport water to all parts of the leaf, and carry food from the leaf to be distributed to other parts of the plant. In a similar way, our veins carry blood, which we need to survive, to our hearts. Take a look at any leaf, especially during the fall, and you can see the veins for yourself.

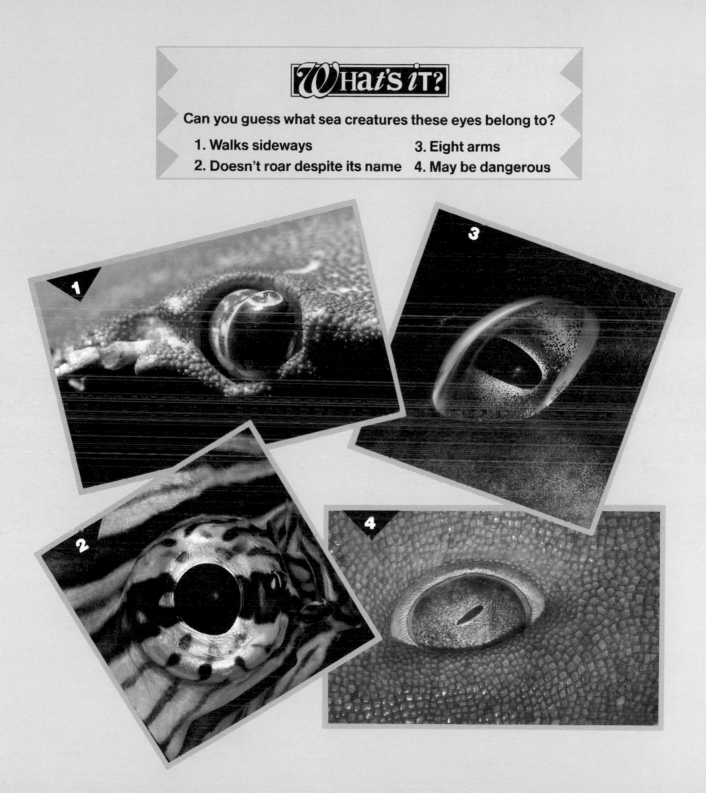

Ｗhat's iT?

Can you guess what sea creatures these eyes belong to?

1. Walks sideways
2. Doesn't roar despite its name
3. Eight arms
4. May be dangerous

5

Answers
and Amazing Facts

FOR PAGE 5

1. GIANT SPIDER CRAB

Giant spider crabs can measure 8 m (26 ft) across when their legs are spread out. That's wider than an average house! Because of their small bodies and long legs, these crabs have poor balance. That's why they live in still waters and hunt slow-moving prey such as other crustaceans, worms and mollusks.

3. OCTOPUS

The lifespan of the octopus is generally only two to four years, and most species mate as soon as they are full grown. The male octopus dies after he has mated. The female octopus lives long enough to brood her young, and then she too dies.

2. LIONFISH

The lionfish is one of the most showy of fishes. Its body, measuring 30.5 cm (12 in) or more, has striped zebralike markings and 13 dorsal fins with poison spines. When disturbed the lionfish spreads and displays its fins. It may attack enemies with its poison spines.

4. NURSE SHARK

Nurse sharks don't usually attack people, although they may bite if they are provoked. But would you believe that the biggest shark in the world attacks only tiny forms of sea life? The whale shark, which can grow to be one and a half times the length of a school bus, eats only plankton and small fish.

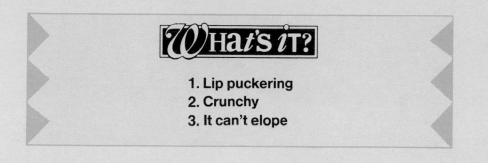

What's it?

1. Lip puckering
2. Crunchy
3. It can't elope

Answers

and

Amazing Facts

FOR PAGE 7

1 LEMON

Lemons have been around for a long time. Chinese records dating from 1175 describe the _li-mung_ as "the size of a small plum…it resembles a small orange and is exceedingly sour to the taste". Lemonade was first mentioned in 1299 as an invention of the Mongolians!

2 APPLE

Grafting helps farmers grow the variety of apples they want. For example, to grow McIntosh apples you can cut a branch from a McIntosh tree, and tie it to the stem of any other apple tree with well-grown roots. When the branch and stem grow together, you remove the older branches of the tree. The tree now produces McIntosh apples from the grafted branch.

3 CANTALOUPE

The name cantaloupe comes from the town of Cantaluppi, in Italy, where the cantaloupe was first grown in Europe. This juicy fruit is a member of the muskmelon family and originally grew in Iran and surrounding areas. The Ancient Egyptians probably relished these melons because pictures of fruit that look like muskmelons appear in their art. The Ancient Greeks used these melons for medicine as well as for food. Christopher Columbus brought muskmelon seeds to the Caribbean in 1494, and from there they were taken to North America.

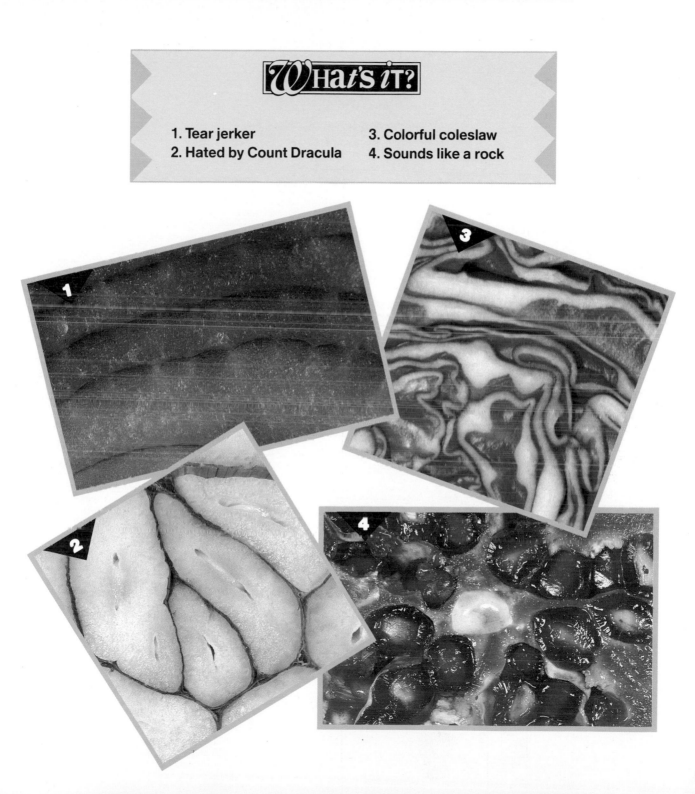

What's it?

1. Tear jerker
2. Hated by Count Dracula
3. Colorful coleslaw
4. Sounds like a rock

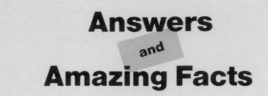

Answers
and
Amazing Facts

FOR PAGE 9

1 RED ONION

The Ancient Egyptians believed that the many-layered onion was a symbol of the universe, and offered it to the gods in their temples. Onions were also fed to the workers who built the pyramids, to give them strength. An average-sized onion has around ten coats or layers.

3 RED CABBAGE

A gardener in England grew a cabbage that weighed over 56 kg (123 lb) and measured 658 cm (259 in) around. That's as big as 50 average-sized cabbages! Relatives of the cabbage include kale, collards, broccoli and cauliflower.

2 GARLIC

Garlic has long been considered a charm and a medicinal herb for healing. It was also fed to the pyramid builders. Some people say you can even use garlic to frighten off vampires (if you believe in them!). A head of garlic contains around 15 cloves, each with its own fine skin.

4 POMEGRANATE

Cut a pomegranate in half and you can see many seeds, each surrounded by a jacket of juicy, crimson flesh. This flesh has a delicious aroma and is refreshing, but a little difficult to eat. The idea is to suck the flesh from the tiny seeds, but some people take the easy way out and swallow the seeds too!

What's it?

Springs from a bulb

What's it?

Unidentified flying object

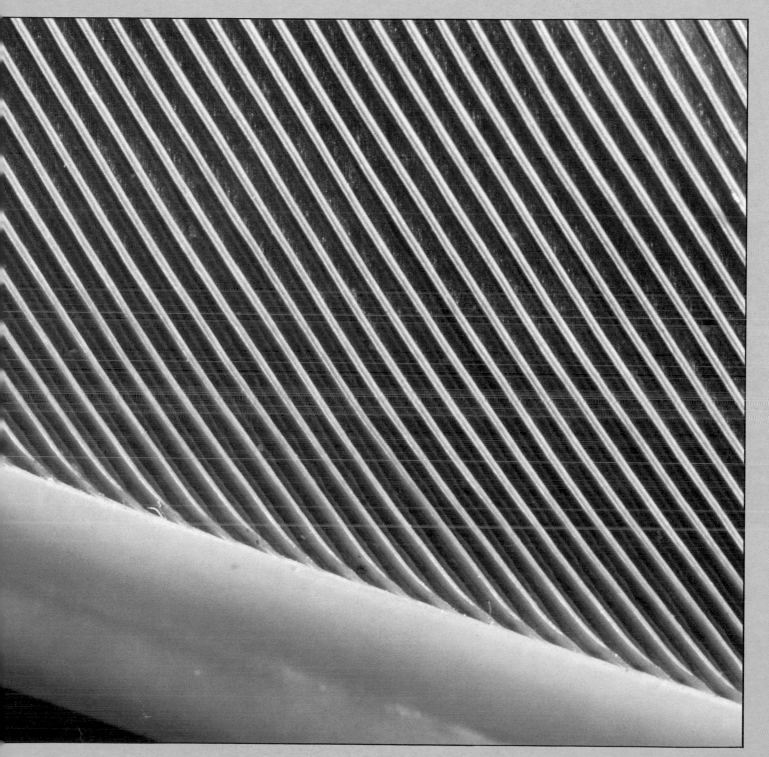

Answers
and
Amazing Facts

FOR PAGE 11 & PAGES 12-13

PAGE 11

DUTCH FAIR TULIP

People started creating new tulip species about 400 years ago, and these novelties sometimes fetched huge sums of money from royal families who wanted them for their gardens! The great-great-great-great grandchildren of these early species of tulip bulbs are still grown today in a bulb museum in Holland. One bulb dating from 1620, the *Lac van Rijn*, was recently used to produce a brand new breed of tulip.

PAGE 12

FEATHER

A feather is a growth of a bird's skin. It is one of the lightest and strongest materials formed by any animal. Scientists believe that feathers evolved from the scales of reptiles during the age of dinosaurs, from 245 to 65 million years ago. Some species of reptiles had scales that were long and loose, and possibly these scales frayed and began to develop into feathers over time. The number of feathers a bird has depends on its species and size. A robin has about 3,000 feathers while a swan has 25,000! There are several different kinds of feathers. Tail feathers attract mates. They also help a bird steer and balance itself. Wing feathers are for flying, and down and body feathers insulate, keeping a bird warm on cold days and cool on hot days.

ꞮꞦHat's it?

1. I make new plants.
2. Pie or lantern
3. Not a good ice-cream holder!

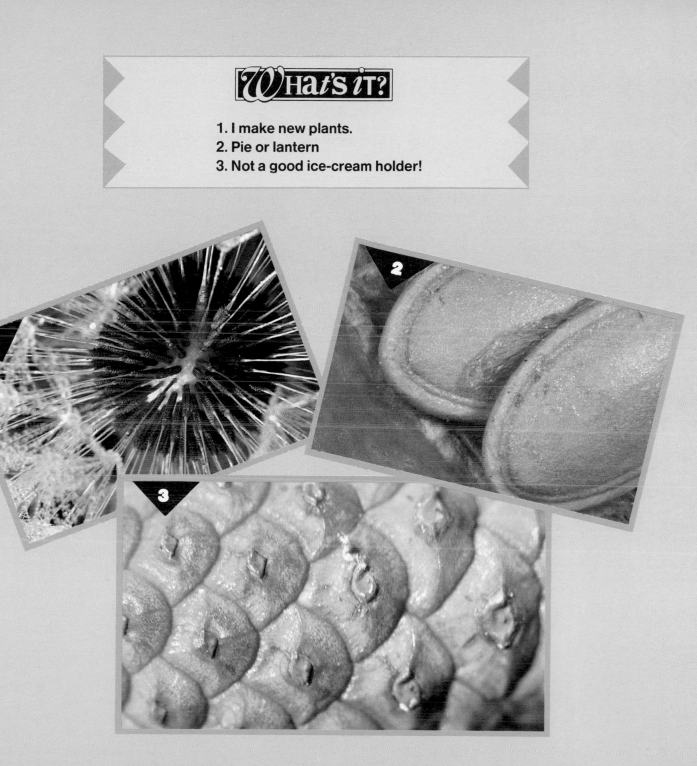

Answers

and

Amazing Facts

FOR PAGE 15

1 DANDELION SEEDS

Dandelion seeds are extremely light and are attached to a cluster of hairs which form a natural parachute. A single dandelion may have as many as 180 of these parachutes. When the wind blows, the parachutes may be carried a long way before the seeds fall into the soil. Then new plants can begin to grow.

2 PUMPKIN SEEDS

Pumpkins, unlike many other fruits we eat, first grew in North America. Wild pumpkins were small and bitter. They were used by the Indians as rattles in ceremonies and dances (when the pumpkin was dried out, the seeds inside rattled). But over time, the Indians began growing pumpkins for food, and gradually they became the sweeter fruit we know today.

3 PINE CONE

This kind of cone is the woody fruit of conifer trees such as pines, firs and spruces. There are over a hundred species of conifers throughout the world, and they all produce cones. Sugar pine cones, which are the largest, can grow 38 cm (15 in) or more. Male cones are covered with many fertile scales that have pollen sacs. These sacs release pollen in spring or early summer. The wind carries the pollen to the scales on female cones, which open to receive it, and then close. Seeds develop between the scales of the female cones then fall to the ground to take root.

What's It?

Here are some nature look-alikes. Only one does not grow.
Can you guess what they are?

Answers and Amazing Facts

FOR PAGE 17

1. WATERMELON BEGONIA

It's easy to see why this popular houseplant is called the watermelon begonia — its silver-striped leaves suggest the markings found on a watermelon. The leaves measure 10 cm (4 in) long and 7.5 cm (3 in) wide, and the plant stands 10-15 cm (4-6 in) tall. It is native to Brazil.

3. STONES

Stones, even those that look perfectly round as though they formed by themselves, are in fact small pieces of broken rock smoothed by time and water. Rock is made up of different mixtures of minerals which can include mica, quartz, calcite, feldspar and many others.

2. LIVING STONES

Living stones are succulent plants that resemble the tiny pebbles among which they grow. They blend into the landscape so well that they cannot be seen by animals that might eat them. They are found in dry areas of southern Africa, and can only be seen easily when they are in bloom.

4. WATERMELON

A watermelon usually weighs from 9-29 kg (20-65 lb) but some have weighed 45 kg (100 lb) — as much as an average-sized 11 year old. Imagine how many people you could feed with a watermelon that size — a hundred people could have a slice! We usually eat watermelon as a thirst quencher on a hot day, but some people use the rind to make pickles and preserves.

What's it?

1. Flutters in the air
2. You won't see this star in the sky.
3. Grows on rocks and trees

Answers

and

Amazing Facts

FOR PAGE 19

1 BUTTERFLY WING

The membrane that forms the broad surface of a butterfly's wing is translucent. Color is contained in a dense covering of scales. The butterfly with the largest wingspan is the *Thysania aggrippina*. Its wingspan measures 30.5 cm (12 in) — about as wide as two handspreads!

2 STARFISH

A starfish does not have a brain. Its body usually consists of five arms located around a central disc. Each arm has two rows of tube feet which the starfish uses to move, breathe and gather food. Its mouth is located on the central disc. A cluster of simple eyes at the tip of each arm helps the starfish distinguish between light and dark.

3 LICHEN

Some lichens form colorful crusts on the surface of rocks, and others cover the bark of trees. They can be found high on the mountains in the Arctic, and in the Antarctic, where other plants can scarcely grow.

Lichens consist of two separate plants: an alga and a fungus. These plants, living attached to each other, form a partnership. The alga contains chlorophyll and provides energy from sunlight, and the fungus provides mineral food and protection (minute woven threads called "hyphae" form a tough skin surrounding the alga).

What's it?

Can you match up these clues with the insects below?

A. Tube unrolls to sip nectar   C. Hair sharp as needles
B. Viselike jaws crush prey   D. Daggerlike mouth parts

Gypsy moth caterpillar
1

Tiger beetle
3

Stiletto fly
2

Cabbage white butterfly
4

Answers

and

Amazing Facts

FOR PAGE 21

1 C. GYPSY MOTH CATERPILLAR

The gypsy moth was brought to North America from Europe in the 1860s. Gypsy moth caterpillars devour the leaves of trees, and they caused serious destruction to orchards and woodlands since they had no natural enemies in their new home. Now many insects, some of them imported from Europe, keep them under better control.

3 B. TIGER BEETLE

Tiger beetles are fast and deadly accurate hunting insects. Even the larva of the tiger beetle is known for its hunting abilities. The larva digs a deep pit in the soil and sits at the entrance. As soon as an insect comes within reach, the larva grabs it with its viselike jaws and drags it into the burrow.

2 D. STILETTO FLY

If you have ever tried to swat a fly buzzing around the house, you know how difficult it is to hit. The fly seems to see you long before you get to it. Flies have eyes made up of thousands of six-sided lenses. Each lens points in a different direction and works independently, so flies are quick to see any movement.

4 A. CABBAGE WHITE BUTTERFLY

Over 1,000 species of butterflies belong to the same family as the cabbage white butterfly. The larvae of some of these species feed on cabbage leaves, hence the name "cabbage white".

What's it?

Loves me, loves me not

Answers
and
Amazing Facts

FOR PAGE 23 & PAGES 24-25

PAGE 23

CECROPIA MOTH CATERPILLAR

The caterpillar of the cecropia moth feeds on leaves and spins a large brownish-gray cocoon. There it changes into a pupa, then into a pretty moth with rust, white and mauve markings against a brown background. These markings look like eyes on its wings, and help frighten away predators. The cecropia is the largest of all North American moths, and you can often see it in late spring and early summer flying about cities.

PAGE 24

CENTER OF DAISY

Two kinds of florets make up a daisy flower. The white petals are called disc florets. They are flat, and direct insects towards the nectar in the center. The inner yellow ones you see are ray florets. They are tubular, and produce nectar. Insects, such as bees, collect nectar to make honey. When a bee collects nectar, pollen grains from the male part of the flower, the anther, stick to its body. And when the bee flies to the next flower, the pollen grains fall onto the female part of the flower, the stigma. Once the pollen grains have landed on the stigma, seeds can be produced. This process is called pollination.

There are two desert plants here.
Can you identify them and their look-alikes?

Answers
and
Amazing Facts

FOR PAGE 27

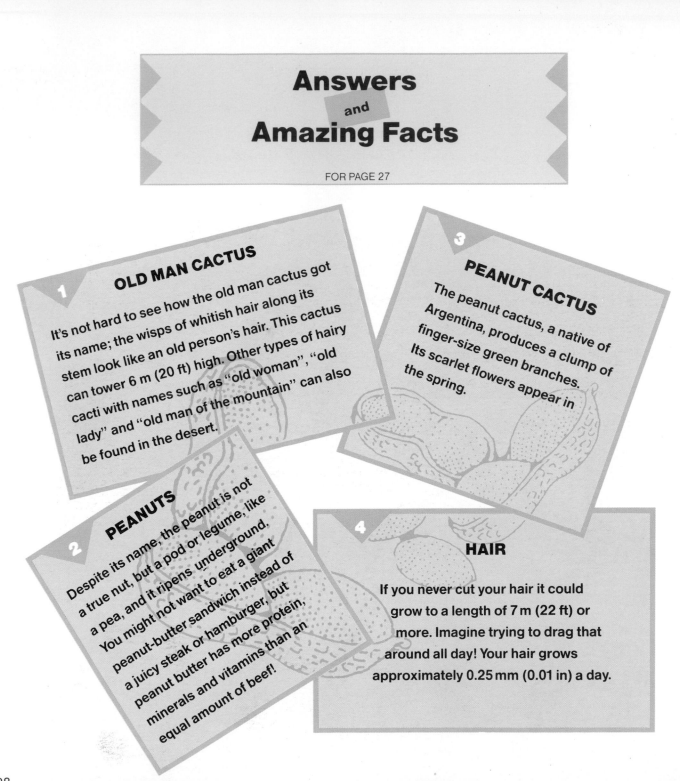

1 OLD MAN CACTUS

It's not hard to see how the old man cactus got its name; the wisps of whitish hair along its stem look like an old person's hair. This cactus can tower 6 m (20 ft) high. Other types of hairy cacti with names such as "old woman", "old lady" and "old man of the mountain" can also be found in the desert.

3 PEANUT CACTUS

The peanut cactus, a native of Argentina, produces a clump of finger-size green branches. Its scarlet flowers appear in the spring.

2 PEANUTS

Despite its name, the peanut is not a true nut, but a pod or legume, like a pea, and it ripens underground. You might not want to eat a giant peanut-butter sandwich instead of a juicy steak or hamburger, but peanut butter has more protein, minerals and vitamins than an equal amount of beef!

4 HAIR

If you never cut your hair it could grow to a length of 7 m (22 ft) or more. Imagine trying to drag that around all day! Your hair grows approximately 0.25 mm (0.01 in) a day.

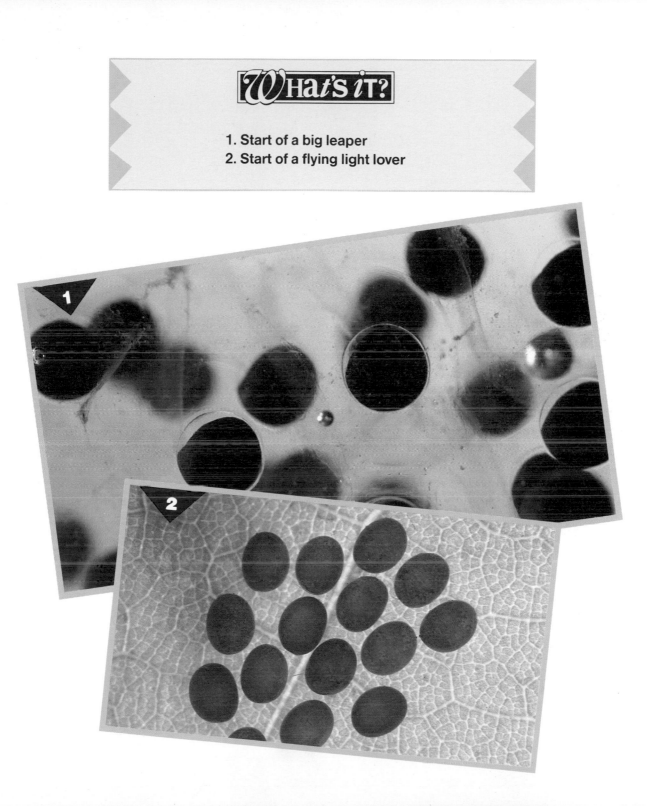

What's iT?

1. Start of a big leaper
2. Start of a flying light lover

Answers

and

Amazing Facts

FOR PAGE 29

FROG EGGS

1

Frogs can lay from 2 to 20,000 eggs at a time, but not all of these survive to become adult frogs. Sometimes eggs and tadpoles are eaten by insects, ducks and fish, or the water they are in dries up. Some species of frogs lay large numbers of eggs and then leave them in or near water, while other species lay only a few eggs and look after them. Many frogs have developed special ways to take care of their eggs. The gray tree frog of South America makes a nest of froth on twigs above water from which the tadpoles drop as they hatch. The female marsupial frog carries her eggs around for three to four months in a pouch on her back, and then releases the tadpoles in shallow water.

MOTH EGGS

2

These eggs belong to the rosy maple moth. As the name suggests, rosy maple moths feed on the leaves of red and silver maples. A female moth can lay from 50 to several thousand eggs. She lays her eggs on the leaf or stem of a plant that she likes to eat. Like most insects, the female moth leaves the eggs to hatch on their own. And like the eggs of other insects which are left to fend for themselves, not all of them survive. Moth eggs vary in shape and color; some are smooth, while others have beautiful sculptured outer coverings.

What's it?

Can you identify these animal backs?

1. Slow and steady
2. Slitherer
3. Champion leaper
4. Independent nature

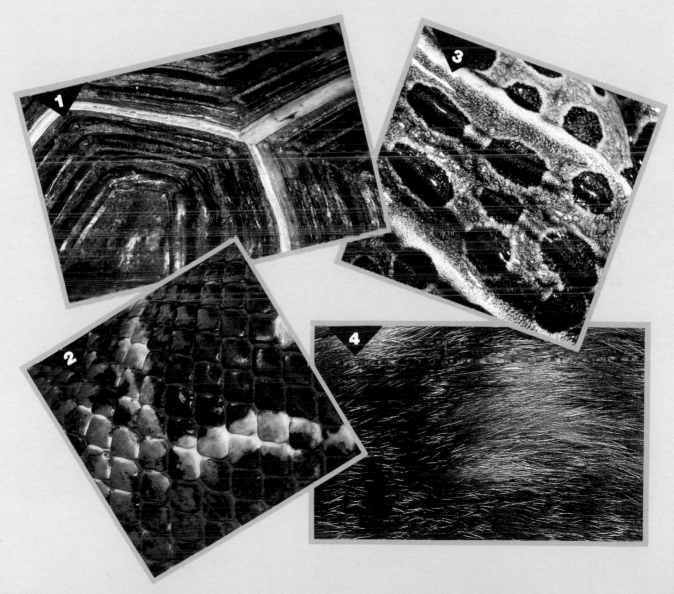

Answers
and
Amazing Facts

FOR PAGE 31

1 TORTOISE

The shell of a tortoise is like armor. It is made up of bones and consists of two parts: a "carapace" covers the animal's back and a "plastron" covers its belly. These parts are connected on each side by a bony bridge. No wonder the tortoise is well protected against predators; it would be hard to sink teeth into a shell like that!

3 LEOPARD FROG

The leopard frog is a medium-sized frog, between 4-8 cm (1½-3 in) long. The largest frog in the world, found in Africa, is the goliath. This monster is, on average, 30.5 cm (12 in) long, although goliaths have measured 41 cm (16 in). That's over twice the size of a robin; imagine one leaping!

2 BOA CONSTRICTOR

The largest boa constrictor on record is 5.6 m (18.5 ft) long. Boa constrictors bite their prey — small mammals such as mice or rats — then they hug them to death. But boas are by no means the largest snakes, and they are not dangerous to humans.

4 CAT

When we are angry we may shout, go red in the face or shake. But when a cat is angry its hair stands on end. A cat's fur consists of guard hairs and shorter underfur. Each guard hair is attached to a muscle that makes it stand up when the cat is angry or frightened. But that doesn't mean that a cat won't "shout" by meowing loudly, or even scratching!